This and That

The Sound of TH

By Peg Ballard

2

This dog
is big.

That dog is small.

This book
is thick.

That book
is thin.

9

This ball is big.

That ball
is small.

14

This pen is thick.

That pen is thin.

17

This box
is big.

That box is small.

21

Word List:

that

thick

thin

this

Note to Parents and Educators

The books in this series are based on current research, which supports the idea that our brains are pattern-detectors rather than rules-appliers. This means children learn to read easier when they are taught the familiar spelling patterns found in English. As children encounter more complex words, they have greater success in figuring out these words by using the spelling patterns.

Throughout the series, the texts allow the reader to practice and apply knowledge of the sounds in natural language. The books introduce sounds using familiar onsets and *rimes*, or spelling patterns, for reinforcement.

For example, the word *cat* might be used to present the short "a" sound, with the letter *c* being the onset and "_at" being the rime. This approach provides practice and reinforcement of the short "a" sound, as there are many familiar words made with the "_at" rime.

The stories and accompanying photographs in this series are based on time-honored concepts in children's literature: well-written, engaging texts and colorful, high-quality photographs combine to produce books that children want to read again and again.

Dr. Peg Ballard
Minnesota State University, Mankato

The Child's World®
childsworld.com

Published by The Child's World®
1980 Lookout Drive • Mankato, MN 56003-1705
800-599-READ • www.childsworld.com

ISBN 9781503819306
LCCN 2016960523

Printed in the United States of America
PA02337

ABOUT THE AUTHOR

Dr. Peg Ballard holds a PhD from Purdue
University and is an associate professor
in the Department of Elementary &
Early Childhood Education at Minnesota
State University, Mankato. Her areas of
expertise are assessment, interventions,
and response to intervention. Dr. Ballard
teaches online graduate courses in the
K–12 reading licensure and master's
program along with reading
interventions in the undergraduate
teacher preparation program.